A River's Journey

Written by Lee Wang
Series Consultant: Linda Hoyt

WorldWise™
Content-based Learning

Contents

Introduction

High in the mountains, there is often a lot of rain, snow and ice.

This is where many rivers start as tiny streams that flow downhill onto flat land. In some places, rivers flow very quickly, and in others, they move very slowly.

As they move, rivers provide food and shelter for many animals, and they make new shapes in the land.

This is the story of the Waikato River, the longest river in New Zealand.

Chapter 1

The journey begins

The snow is melting, and trickles of water run quickly down the side of the mountain. They join together to become a fast-moving stream that will become bigger and stronger as it flows downhill.

This is the beginning of the river's journey.

Waterfalls

As the water falls over tall rocks or a **cliff**, a **waterfall** is formed. Pieces of rock are swept along by the water and carried over the waterfall.

Kingfishers nest high in the trees or on cliff banks and dive down to catch crayfish and small fish in their beaks.

Find out more

What is the nearest river to where you live?

Gorges and canyons

As the river flows downhill, it carries large and small rocks with it. The rocks tumble around in the water, crashing into other rocks and moving mud or sand from the bottom and sides of the river.

The river makes a deep **valley** with **steep** walls called a gorge. A gorge can become a **canyon** that slowly gets wider and deeper as the river wears away the rock.

Wild goats, red deer and sheep live in the forests that grow on top of the gorges.

Chapter 2

Winding across the plains

When the river leaves the mountains and gorges, it winds across flat land called plains. Here, the water moves more slowly.

Sandy banks

On the plains, small streams flow into the river, and it becomes wider and deeper. Sandy banks form along the sides of the river as it winds across the plains.

The Pacific black duck eats plants, snails and insects in these parts of the river.

Floodplains and lakes

When there is a lot of rain, the river floods, and water flows over the banks. Floods dump sand and mud that make a low, flat area, called a floodplain.

Sometimes, as the river bends and curves, water can get cut off. This cut-off water forms a lake that is separate from the river.

The giant Kokopu fish and black mudfish live in the water on the floodplain. Swans, herons and bitterns live on the lakes.

Find out more

What kind of birds live on rivers and lakes near you?

13

Chapter 3
Meeting the sea

Deltas

Close to the sea, the river leaves behind the mud and sand it has carried along. It forms a swampy **delta** made up of many channels.

Many types of birds feed on the crabs and shrimp that live in the shallow water of the delta. These birds have webbed feet that help them to **wade** through the mud and sand.

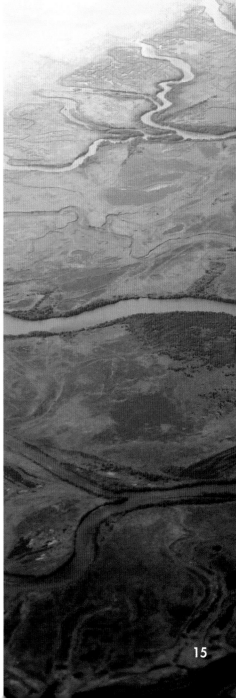

As the river gets closer to the sea it widens and forms an **estuary**. The river water and the sea water mix together, as the river flows into the sea.

Conclusion

The river started high in the mountains, then moved across low, flat land to the sea. Many animals lived and found food along the river.

As the river moved, it changed shape many times, and it also made amazing new shapes in the land.

Glossary

canyon   a deep valley with steep, rocky walls, usually with a river or stream running through it

cliff   a high, steep, rocky piece of land

delta   an area of land shaped like a fan, found where a river runs into the sea

dive   to fly downward, quickly and suddenly

estuary   a body of shallow water where a river meets the sea

steep   a slope that is almost straight up and down

valley   usually flat land found in between mountains or hills

wade   to walk through something such as water or mud, that makes moving difficult

waterfall   the part of a river where water falls from a high place

Index